Chopsticks!
An Owner's Manual

Hashi-San

Illustrations by Michael Hofmann

Conari Press
Berkeley, CA

This book would not have existed
without the generous help of:

Kim Hun, Chris Jay, Bao-chin Lin Jochim, Chris Jochim
Hiroshi Komoda, Eiko Shibuya Madson, Jack Madson

Printed in the United States of America on recycled paper

Cover by Andrea Sohn Design. Cover illustration by Tina Cash

ISBN: 0-943233-23-2

Library of Congress Cataloging-in-Publication Data

Hashi-San, 1948-
     Chopsticks! : an owner's manual / Hashi-San : illustrations by Michael Hofmann.
         p. cm.
     ISBN 0-943233-23-2 : $6.95
     1. Chopsticks—History. 2. Asia—Civilization. 3. Food habits—Asia. I. Title.
GT2949.H37 1991
642'.7—dc20   91-25122
                                                CIP

Chopsticks!

Author's Note

Why a book on chopsticks?

Most of my friends giggle when I tell them I've written a book about chopsticks. After all, how much can you say about two small pieces of wood?

The surprising truth is quite a lot. Chopsticks are not merely eating implements. They are useful tools that are intricately woven into the fabric of Chinese, Japanese, Korean and Vietnamese culture. Chopsticks have played a crucial role in world politics, religion, economics, social reform, tradition, and the development of what gourmets recognize as some of the most exquisite of world cuisines.

Restaurant hopping is a passion for many of us. But how often do we use dining out as an opportunity to learn about world culture? *CHOPSTICKS* is intended to help you experience the flavor of Asian cultures as well as the food. It was fun to write and I hope fun to read.

Read it the next time you sit down to Sizzling Rice Soup or Beef Teriyaki.

Enjoy!

In the Beginning . . .

The birth of chopsticks can be viewed only through the mist of myth and legend. But we do know that in the beginning there were only knives and fingers. As legend has it, two poor farmers who had been thrown off their land and out of their village for some long-forgotten transgression, travelled throughout the China in despair. Hounded wherever they went, unwelcome in village after village, tired and hungry, they eventually succumbed to temptations and stole a hunk of meat from a storeroom in a small village.

The two farmers-turned-thieves ran from the village and deep into the neighboring forest and hastily built a fire to cook their meal. As the aroma of roasting meat overcame the patience of our starving heros, they snatched up twigs from the forest floor and used then to rip still-sizzling pieces of meat from the fire and into their trembling mouths. And so began the the long and illustrious history of chopsticks.

The use of chopsticks began slowly and then picked up steam. Some claim that the explosion of chopsticks in twelfth-century China can better be traced to the desperate need, poetically stated in this twelfth-century poem, to set a table for a visiting friend enemy without the presence of a threatening knife.

The Second Autumn Empress

You ask me to your table
And yet your knife you point
Directly at my chest
As though urging me to duel.
Why, then I have no business to be
Sitting at your table—
Let's rather meet on the battlefield,
Where no one tries to conceal
That it is his only wish
To insult an adversary.
                    —Ancient Chinese Poem

Confucius Says

The rapid spread of chopsticks throughout ancient China is sometimes credited to Confucius, who wrote that "the honorable man allows no knives at his table." Confucius, who was a committed vegetarian, did not think it proper that instruments of slaughter should be a part of dining. Those who followed his advice soon realized that, out of necessity, a table without knives became a table with chopsticks.

Forks, Fingers, and Chopsticks

*N*ot a lot of us have spent time contemplating the manner in which food is consumed around the world, but it is a matter of great import. In the beginning, of course, there were just fingers. Indeed billions and billions of meals went by before it occurred to our ancestors that something other than fingers could be used to eat with. According to archeologists, the next utensil was more than likely a stone knife, although an argument could be made that the big stick used by our cave-dwelling ancestors to twirl a chunk of meat over a fire was a distant relative of a chopstick.

Around three thousand years ago, the Chinese began using chopsticks while the rest of the world was still content to eat with their hands. And it was only a few hundred years ago

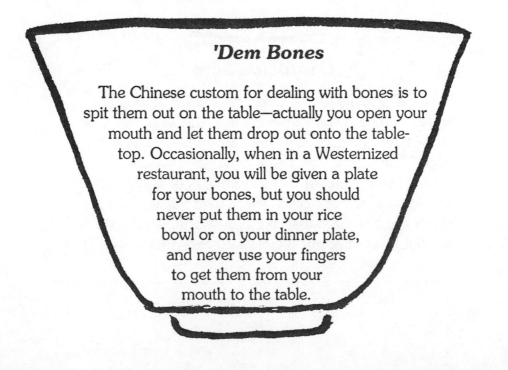

'Dem Bones

The Chinese custom for dealing with bones is to spit them out on the table—actually you open your mouth and let them drop out onto the table-top. Occasionally, when in a Westernized restaurant, you will be given a plate for your bones, but you should never put them in your rice bowl or on your dinner plate, and never use your fingers to get them from your mouth to the table.

Great Western Gaffe

The rice plate—a plate of rice topped with a sauce or stir-fried combination—is a Western concoction, one that can cause problems for chopstick wielders. In the East, rice is put in a bowl that can conveniently be raised to your mouth for easy chopsticks transfer.

This process is frequently assisted by the glutinous texture of the rice—making it relatively easy to get from bowl to mouth. But rice plates, particularly rice plates with non-sticky, long-grain rice, can be near impossible to get from plate to mouth with a pair of chopsticks without leaving a trail of rice across the table. So next time ask for your rice in a bowl.

in Western Europe that forks and spoons were teamed with knives; the combination proved popular and soon conquered a large cross section of the globe.

Today, the world is pretty evenly divided up into three camps: those who eat with their hands, as in India, Africa, and across much of the Mid-East; those who eat with chopsticks, found mainly in China, Japan, Korea, and Vietnam; and those who eat using a knife, fork, and spoon, as those in Europe, the Americas, Australia, and New Zealand do.

The categories are of course an over-simplification since both hand-eaters and chopstick wielders use knives to prepare their food; some chopstick adherents also use a spoon, and of course everybody—even though it is sometimes done furtively—continues to use his hands. But as a central cultural system for attacking food, the hand/chopstick/fork division stands up well.

The Good, the Bad
and the Slippery?

While cultural pride usually forces us all to view our particular approach as the one that is obviously superior, there are in fact distinct advantages and disadvantages to all three.

Hand-eaters have the obvious advantage of not needing to worry about selecting, purchasing, storing, cleaning, or transporting eating utensils. And they are always armed and ready to snack without having to hunt down the proper tools. Hand-eaters also insist that the direct physical contact with food allows you to better experience the full joy of a meal with all its temperatures and textures.

The disadvantage is obvious—a considerable amount of energy must be spent getting and keeping hands clean. And most hand-eaters are figuratively forced to eat with one hand tied behind their backs; virtually all hand-eaters are appalled by anyone who would eat with the left hand. That one is reserved for other matters.

The advantages of the marriage of the knife, spoon, and fork are both ease of use (as long as you aren't asked to follow the Emily Post rules of order) and the great variety of different food presentations that can be successfully attacked. The size and shape of food are truly of no consequence.

The main drawback is well known to those of us who use the utensil trio—the prospect of sitting at a formal dinner with four forks, three spoons, four knives, and not one single clue as to which to use for what.

Chopstick users enjoy numerous advantages. They avoid the problem of sticky hands after dinner; and the already oppressed left-handed population is allowed to eat with their dominant hand rather than throw food all over the rest of us while trying to master the right-handed technique.

Chopsticks have the clear advantage over forks, knives, and spoons as they are a one-handed implement, ready to fly out over the dishes of food and snatch a morsel for instant and elegant gratification. And adherents also claim that chopsticks allow for the ultimate in a well-contemplated and appreciated meal since they require you to savor each individual morsel and will not allow you to shovel food down your throat.

The main disadvantage of chopsticks is that you are given the terrible choice at a very young age of starving to death or learning how to make your first pair of chopsticks function well enough to get at least a subsistence level of food into your mouth.

A second disadvantage is that the use of chopsticks requires that all food be reduced to relatively small pieces. (This is probably one of the major reasons why only three people in the Midwest have been documented as truly proficient in the use of chopsticks—big steaks and the two little sticks just don't go together.)

Romantic Interludes

It is ancient Chinese folk-wisdom that you can tell who someone will marry by how she grips her chopsticks. The closer down toward the tip of the chopstick she holds it, the closer will live her spouse; the farther up the chopstick, the farther away his bride will come from. In a society of small villages, such information could obviously be of invaluable use to the young men and women of marrying age.

A Sticky Issue

With the discovery of a pair of ivory chopsticks in the ruins of an eleventh-century B.C. palace of the Zhou dynasty in China, it became clear that the Chinese began their commitment to chopsticks more than three thousand years ago. But why chopsticks?

First, the use of chopsticks allowed diners to eat meals still steaming hot from the fire. With the aid of chopsticks to lift the sizzling food from pot to mouth, for the first time in human history people could eat their meals at a temperature dictated by the mouth and not the hands.

The real key to the widespread use of chopsticks in China, however, is more than likely found in the heartbreakingly small percentage of China's massive landmass that can actually support agriculture. With precious little arable land, the Chinese have made an art out of preparing and eating virtually every part of everything that grows or moves. Such a creative approach, however, often dictates considerable preparation in order to render otherwise inedible elements not just edible but delicious.

In short, food needed to be cooked.

That, however, brought up another serious problem—fuel. China not only faced a never-ending food shortage, it faced an even more serious scarcity of fuel. Cooking had to be squeezed into the shortest possible time frame in order to minimize the expenditure of precious fuel.

The obvious solution was to reduce everything to small, quickly cooked, bite-sized pieces *before* lighting the precious fire; bite-sized pieces were perfectly suited to be transferred to the mouth by chopsticks.

Tests of Skill

For children, learning to use chopsticks is more difficult than mastering a fork, but there is compensation—challenging your friends to chopstick competitions. Two of the more difficult tasks—to be performed entirely with chopsticks and without any assistance from fingers—is peeling the shell off a cooked shrimp and eating Mu Shu Pork, which is a stir-fry mixture rolled into a tortilla-like pancake.

The Imperial Chinese Kitchen

Records from the earliest days of the Han dynasty circa 200 B.C. list as "kitchen help" for the emperor: 2,271 employees including 128 everyday chefs; 128 more chefs reserved for banquets; 335 grain, vegetable, and fruit specialists; 162 dieticians; 94 ice men; 62 pickle and sauce chefs; and 62 salt men.

Naming the Sticks

𝒯he earliest written name for chopsticks is found in the ancient *Li Ji,* or *Book of Rites.* It is the Chinese character that depicts a happy man holding two pieces of bamboo. The character was related to the word *help* but the pronunciation of the word ("zhou") was too close to the sound of the word for *stop* for the likes of the Chinese boat people.

Throughout Chinese history these unfortunate souls, who literally lived and died on the junks that plied the waters of China's great rivers, were cruelly discriminated against, but they made their mark in history by renaming chopsticks *kuai zi.* Roughly translated as "fast children" or "quick little boys," the name with its fortunate connotations was quickly adopted throughout China, while the written character remained the same as before.

The English name of chopsticks arose out of a blurred

Chopstick Imperialism?

Why chopsticks were adopted throughout China Korea, Japan and Vietnam, but never spread to Cambodia or Thailand is puzzling to many. The probable reason is that the history of both countries—situated as they are between the two giants of India and China—was a constant struggle to maintain a separate and distinct identity. One aspect of that resistance appears to have been a refusal to use chopsticks, even though both countries have sizable Chinese populations who provide a daily example of the ease and elegance of chopstick use.

attempt to translate this Chinese name; chop, chop being the pidgin English phrase for "quickly" or "fast," *quick little boys* turned into the word *chopsticks.*

The Japanese accepted certain things Chinese, including many Chinese words, but from the outset they devised their own name for the wonderful eating utensil from China—they called them *hashi.* The exact origins of the word are lost, but one theory is that since the first Japanese chopsticks were tweezer-like, they reminded the users of a bird's beak (*kuchi bashi,* shortened to *hashi*). Another explanation is that the ends of the tweezers-style chopsticks had to be brought together, and the word *end* is also *hashi.* More commonly accepted, perhaps for its lyrical quality, is the explanation that chopsticks are the bridge from plate to mouth (and metaphorically the bridge from man to god) and thus *hashi,* which is the word for "*bridge,*" became hashi the chopstick.

Both the Koreans and the Vietnamese took a more straightforward path—the Korean word (pronounced "*ceqkalak*") and the Vietnamese word (*dua*)—simply mean "chopsticks."

Korean Origins

The earliest appearance of chopsticks in Korea may never be known, but Korean folk historians insist that the near-mythical founder of the Ki-ja dynasty, Ki-ja himself, introduced chopsticks to Korea as early as 1050 B.C. Such an early arrival is certainly possible since Ki-ja actually began his life as Chi-tzu, a brilliant minister and distant relative of Chou Hsin, the last emperor of the Shang dynasty.

As a faithful minister, Chi-tzu warned the emperor that his practice of worrying more about devising new tricks for his dancing girls than concerning himself with the growing misery of his people was certain to lose him his empire. Chi-tzu was rewarded for such advice by being placed in an altogether unpleasant imperial prison.

When, as Chi-tzu predicted, the Shang dynasty did fall, Wu Wang, the founder of the new Zhou dynasty, promptly freed Chi-tzu out of respect for his faithful service to his discredited and recently deceased relative. However, Chi-tzu did not believe it proper to switch allegiance so quickly; with the gracious permission of the new emperor, Chi-tzu crossed over into Korea. There he became known as Ki-ja, the founder of the first lasting dynasty in Korean history, one that continued in one fashion or another until 193 B.C.

Since we know from sound archeological evidence that a pair of ivory chopsticks was found within the tomb of one of the early Zhou emperors, it is certainly conceivable that as Chi-tzu made the journey to become Ki-ja, one of the items he brought with him was a pair of chopsticks.

Scholarly Chopsticks

Koreans believe that the first pair of chopsticks arrived in the pocket of the national hero Ki-ja just over three thousand years ago. Whether it did or not, the spread of chopsticks to the table of farmer and merchant undoubtedly took many more years to accomplish. It wasn't the problem of teaching a nation how to use chopsticks that slowed the progress, it was more a problem of finding the nation.

In the thousand years or so after the arrival of Ki-ja from China, Korea went through the growing pains of a country. Native tribes of one area would get together with a tribe from another area usually to make mischief upon still another tribe. Bows and arrows were more the implement of the day than chopsticks. What was to become Korea was, through most of the last thousand years B.C., a place with no political unity and no common language.

However, being attached to China had pretty much sealed Korea's future development, and over time every major advancement or curiosity that blossomed in China made its way down the Korean peninsula. While it is difficult to pinpoint a particular time when a critical mass of Koreans mastered the art of eating with sticks, the most likely time frame is somewhere between the brief but dramatic rule of the Ch'in dynasty in China (around 200 B.C.) and the middle of the early Han dynasty (around 100 B.C.).

The great Ch'in emperor, Shih Huang-ti, is most commonly known as the builder of the Great Wall, but among his lesser accomplishments was the initiation of history's first large-scale book-burning campaign. Shih Huang-ti felt too much attention was being paid to China's already ancient history and not enough to his glorious reign, but the net effect of his tyranny was a major migration of Chinese scholars down the Korean peninsula. Undoubtedly, along with their scrolls and writing implements went many a fine pair of chopsticks.

Barely one hundred years later the newly installed Chinese Han dynasty occupied the northern reaches of Korea and no doubt made certain that the locals were all developing proper chopsticks technique. In one of the great mysteries of history, that brief period of Chinese control was the only serious attempt by China to colonize Korea, which later had to endure the incursion of the Japanese from the south.

Chopsticks Conquer Vietnam

Vietnam has always been somewhat of a mystery to historians, specifically how the Vietnamese managed, after nearly one thousand years of Chinese rule, to resist being swallowed up into Chinese culture like so many before them. First conquered by the Han warrior emperor, Han Wu-ti, in 111 B.C., Vietnam was made a province of China and was administered under the classic Chinese system of government until A.D. 938 when Ngo Quyen took advantage of the collapsing T'ang dynasty to drive the Chinese out of Vietnam.

During the long occupation, Vietnam adopted many of the beneficial aspects of Chinese civilization, including the consummate skill at taming great rivers and carving out productive, well-irrigated rice fields, the iron ploughshare, their system of writing, their ardent Buddhism, and the custom of eating with chopsticks. At least sometimes.

Unlike in China and Japan, chopsticks were never granted a large role in Vietnamese ceremonial or social life, and aren't even used consistently as utensils.

The Warrior Queens

Two of Vietnam's greatest legendary heros were warrior queens, sisters Trung Trac and Trung Nhi, who succeeded briefly in A.D. 39 in overthrowing the Chinese and ruling jointly for four years until the Chinese returned. Facing certain defeat, the sisters drowned themselves rather than submit to their hated enemies. They remain today a symbol of Vietnamese resistance to foreign oppression.

Chopsticks Sail to Japan

Through its strategic placement between China and Japan, Korea became the often-reluctant cultural highway between the two. Throughout the first few centuries A.D., much of the rich cultural production of China made its way down the Korean peninsula and then by boat across the 180-kilometer Straits of Korea, and ultimately into the hands of the early Japanese imperial court.

No one is certain exactly when the first pair of chopsticks made the passage to Japan; however, having made the long journey, chopsticks were initially treated as precious objects and were more than likely used

China

Vietnam

exclusively in religious ceremonies. By the fifth century, chopsticks had already found their way to a place of honor in a daily ceremony to the Shinto sun god. The Japanese emperor had built a shrine to the sun god in Ise Jingu, and a ceremonial meal was served each morning and evening with the assistance of a pair of pure white chopsticks made from the willow tree.

The Origins of Confusion

Not everything that Japan borrowed from China worked out as well as chopsticks. Around the fifth century—approximately the same time as the introduction of chopsticks—the Japanese borrowed the Chinese character alphabet. They should have given it back. Today Japanese is written in at least three and often four different alphabets causing untold hardship on schoolchildren and prompting one noted historian to say that written Japanese is "the least efficient language system in the world."

Noble Sticks

Shotoko Taishi is a considered by many historians to be the greatest figure in early Japanese history. He ruled as regent from A.D. 593 until his death in 622, and is credited with having written the first Japanese constitution and establishing the first truly centralized government in Japan.

But perhaps one of his most important accomplishments was the sending of Japanese ambassadors to China. Beginning in the year 600, the regent prince initiated the direct contact with China that would ultimately change the history of Japan profoundly. At the time, Chinese ideas had made an appearance in Japan—Buddhism was officially introduced in A.D. 522, Chinese characters had been adopted by some early scribes as early as the fourth century, and chopsticks had made their way into the religious ceremonies—but these were virtually unknown outside ruling and religious circles.

Imaginary Chopsticks

The earliest chopsticks found in Japan were made of one continuous piece of bamboo—joined at the top—so they looked like tweezers. The Japanese name for these was *maboroshi no hashi,* or imaginary chopsticks. Although this attempt to create Japanese-style chopsticks was doomed to extinction by the tenth century, it is an early demonstration of the Japanese talent of accepting the cultural gifts of other countries and adapting them in their own fashion. The Japanese finally abandoned the tweezer-style chopsticks and settled for the now-familiar, thin, pointed version.

With Shotoko Taishi's reign, however, the importance of all things Chinese increased dramatically, including the role of chopsticks. Just as he began to remake the traditional tribal nature of Japanese society into a centralized government on the Chinese model, so too he officially adopted the use of chopsticks at all government functions. Under Shotoko Taishi, chopsticks began their transformation from primarily an object of religious significance to the commonest of eating tools. Japan's love affair with chopsticks had begun in earnest.

Chopstick Power

The undisputed oldest wooden building in the world is the Golden Hall of the Horyu-ji Temple at Ise, Japan, built by Shotoko Taishi in the year 607. Designed in the fashion of the then-glorious T'ang dynasty temples, the Golden Hall, with its daily traditional chopstick offerings, has outlived them all. Japan is the only country that integrated chopsticks into its religious ceremonies; perhaps the gods' appreciation of chopsticks has helped preserve the Golden Hall.

Marco Polo's Chopsticks

Unfortunately, history does not record the occasion of the first chopsticks to reach the West, but it is likely that the bearer of that original pair was none other than the famous wandering Venetian merchant, Marco Polo. In the early part of the thirteenth century Marco Polo, along with his father and uncle, spent twenty years travelling throughout China attached to the imperial court of Kublai Khan. Throughout that time, Marco Polo was an honored guest at countless banquets and even was appointed as the ruler of a large Chinese city for a short period of time. By the thirteenth century, chopsticks were firmly established throughout most parts of China, and there is no doubt that they were a regular part of the merchant's day; so there's little doubt that he came to be quite proficient with chopsticks.

It is curious therefore that no mention of chopsticks appeared in Polo's lengthy accounts of his travels, although he also made no mention of the Great Wall of China which, according to his itinerary, he crossed over more than seven times. Perhaps his comment, written in the book of his travels, that "I only wrote down half of what I saw" was more true than we can imagine. What he did write down, however, got him into enough trouble.

Marco Polo returned to Venice in the year 1295 after completing what would go down in history as one of the most remarkable journeys of all times, but his reception was not what one might have expected. His fantastic tales of the glorious wonders of the East were simply too much for his countrymen to believe. He died the object of ridicule, and for centuries the name Marco Polo was used to refer to a teller of wild tales.

Whether Marco Polo ever attempted to demonstrate the use of chopsticks to any of his countrymen is not recorded, but his lack of persistence may have ultimately saved the day for the Western use of knives, forks, and spoons, since forks did not come into fashion until nearly a century after Marco Polo's return.

Hold The Pasta

Marco Polo is commonly credited with introducing pasta to Italy from China. He didn't; the Italians had been making pasta for some time already. The confusion apparently comes from a reference in his account of a wheat and water "paste" that was cooked and eaten by some of the nomad tribes he met along his route.

China's Common Pot

Which came first, chopsticks or a cuisine peculiarly suited to chopsticks? The answer is lost in antiquity, but clearly the expanding use of chopsticks had a profound influence on the refinement of Chinese cooking and can in many ways be seen as the formative influence in what has become one of the great culinary traditions of the world.

The Chinese eat with chopsticks and a spoon, abandoning any use of the knife at the table. This arrangement dictates that all food be prepared in small, bite-sized morsels. That in turn imposed a heavy emphasis on preparation—chopping, slicing, and marinating (to tenderize the more difficult-to-digest ingredients)—and determined certain cooking styles to assure a balanced flavoring.

Out of this emerged what became the centerpiece not only of Chinese cooking but of the family social structure as well—the emphasis on the common pot. Very early in Chinese history, the family meal consisted of individual bowls of grains (millet in the north and rice in the south) with a pot of stew. This was cooked in a *ge-cauldron* over a pit fire; the stew simmered on the bottom while the grains cooked in a clay steamer set over the stew.

When the meal was ready, everyone would gather around with their chopsticks, be served a bowl of millet or rice, and reach into the cauldron to pluck out the pieces of stew. The meal would be finished off—with the help of the traditional Chinese spoon—by consuming the stewy liquid.

Two thousand years and a proliferation of dishes later, the basic structure of a Chinese meal remains the same: a bowl of rice is in front of each participant, who is armed with chopsticks and the flat-bottomed Chinese spoon and shares a number of bite-sized foods from communal pots with the other members of the family.

Soybeans—From Pauper to Prince

Prior to the culinary renaissance of the Han dynasty (200 B.C.), having nothing but soybeans to chew and water to drink was the mark of true poverty. But soybean farmers had the distinct advantage of producing healthy crops even in poor soil and bad years. Eventually the hidden versatility of the soybean was discovered, and today, from bean milk and sprouts to soy sauce and tofu, the soybean has become a prince of Chinese cuisine.

Chop Chop

*C*hopsticks may dictate the size of pieces of food in China, but a country's particular agriculture, animal husbandry, and cultural traditions control the rest of the cuisine. The Chinese are unsurpassed in their pursuit of culinary excellence and have an astounding assortment of dishes.

For all its variety of cuisines, the basic tools of the Chinese kitchen are remarkably simple: the wok, a cleaver, a steamer, a ladle, and a strainer. Most Chinese cooking takes place rapidly (to preserve scarce fuel) and the workhorse of the kitchen is the amazing wok. Its tapered sides and rounded bottom make for a rapid, even, and wide dispersal of heat from the fire, allowing the bite-sized ingredients to be stir-fried quickly and promoting the rapid boiling of liquids.

Yin & Yang

The Chinese believe that all meals must include yin and yang. Yin represents the cool, moist, female characteristics, represented in such food as asparagus, mushrooms, and most fruits. Yang foods, like peppers, garlic, deep-fried foods, and ginger embody the hot, dry, strong, male characteristics.

Cutting and chopping are the key elements in preparation, and Chinese cooking includes ten cutting techniques that result in eleven classic shapes—all designed to be readily plucked out of the pot by a pair of chopsticks. Most of these shapes are familiar to Western cooks—cube, julienne, mince, etc.—but why the gear shape should emerge as one of the eleven is lost in culinary history.

The gear shape most frequently makes its appearance in as a dumpling in soups, and looks just like it sounds—round with a series of squared "teeth" running around the perimeter.

The Gang of Four Flavors

China is a huge country, and the cuisine is customarily broken down into four regional categories, although there is considerable disagreement as to where the boundaries lie.

The northern cuisine, sometimes called Mandarin or Peking cooking, is centered in the heart of ancient Chinese civilization and benefitted from centuries of the best chefs of China migrating to the imperial capital. Probably because of the imperial presence the best-known dishes (such as Peking Duck) tend toward a more regal bearing. The basic ingredients emphasize wheat products over rice, with noodles, dumplings, and steamed breads predominating, and scallions, leeks, and sweet bean sauce as the most common accompaniments. Famous dishes include Mu Shu Pork, Rice Crusted Soup, and Scallion Pancakes.

The southern cuisine, centered in Canton, is by far the best known outside China due to the large numbers of chefs

Noodle Know-How

In China, wheat had always been a poor cousin to the preferred grains, millet and rice. But with the importation of the flour mill from the West in the early days of the Han dynasty, even the poorest of peasants could grind flour to make a new delicacy—noodles. Always quick to honor a new way of eating, by the end of the Han period in A.D. 200, noodles were regular fare at imperial banquets.

who emigrated to Western countries from that area. Blessed with a subtropical climate in the heart of the rice belt and easy access to the sea, southerners always had more to work with than their cousins elsewhere in China. Cantonese preparations emphasize color and subdued spices—primarily plum sauce, hoisin sauce, and soy sauce—and both peanut and sesame oil are key elements. Famous dishes include Sweet Roast Pork, Won Tons, Suckling Pig, Shark Fin Soup, and stir-fried anything.

The eastern region is centered in the massive port of Shanghai, and is often considered the poor cousin of Chinese cuisine. Chefs of the eastern school rely heavily on soy sauce and sugar for flavorings; dishes often include bamboo shoots and a variety of seafood. Sweet-and-sour recipes are common to this area as well as Drunken Chicken and Honey Ham.

The western region, which includes Szechuan and Hunan cooking, is dominated by richly flavored and spicy foods with lots of anise pepper and garlic. The area is also well known for fresh-fish dishes and the contrast of hot, sweet, and sour presentations. Famous dishes include Hot-and-Sour Soup, Szechuan Pork, and Vegetables Coated in Garlic Sauce.

Soy Sauce Secrets

Soy sauce was a late-blooming addition to the Chinese kitchen (sometime around 100 B.C.), but has since become the staple on every Chinese table. Soy sauce is made by steaming soybeans until they are soft and then mashing them together with wheat flour. This paste is then molded into squares, salted, and placed in a crock to ferment for forty days. The liquid that is drained off is soy sauce.

Dining, Korean Style

While the Koreans readily took to chopsticks, they rejected the short, flat-bottomed Chinese spoon in favor of their own unique version, traditionally a long-handled brass spoon about ten inches long with a shallow round body. And while the Chinese spoon was reserved for soups, historically the Korean spoon was used for virtually everything, and chopsticks were a strictly supplemental utensil.

The use of the spoon has diminished in recent years relative to chopsticks, but it still serves the Korean diner well. For example, rice, an always troublesome grain to eat with chopsticks despite its central role in Asian cooking, is still customarily eaten with a spoon.

The Koreans also rejected the Chinese theory of gathering together around the central pot. Indeed, the Koreans have eliminated the dining area altogether. They eat instead at separate low tables that are set up anywhere in the house that is convenient.

Traditionally, a Korean meal unfolded over time and

Korean Soy Sauce

The Korean version of soy sauce manages to capture all the essential flavors of Korea. To make your own, add to some store-bought light soy sauce to taste: chopped onions, roasted sesame seeds, sesame oil, crushed garlic, a little vinegar, a touch of sugar, and a pinch of chili.

space. First the grandfather and father would be served on their separate tables, often in separate rooms. Then tables for the women and children would be set. Everyone was expected to eat in respectful silence. Even today most Korean homes lack a dining area and even when meals are eaten together, the family tends to be spread out and maintains a silent respect.

A Passion for Garlic

The Koreans are famous for their liberal use of garlic—including the delicious pickled garlic shoots. But not all Asian cuisines fully appreciate garlic—the Japanese ignore it completely. No one knows if garlic has always been frowned upon, but the earliest Zen monks believed that garlic increased the passions of anyone who ate it, and at least for monks who were striving to rid themselves of all human desires, it was strictly off-limits. Even today you can see large stone posts in front of Zen monastery gates inscribed with the words, "no sake or garlic can enter this gate."

The Korean Kitchen

The cuisine of Korea, while bearing a distant relationship to that of China and served in a manner similar to Japanese food, differs distinctively from either, with a particular emphasis on sweet foods, hot-peppery spices, garlic, and pickled vegetables.

The Korean kitchen is perhaps the closest to the Chinese in the heavy reliance on the *sot*—the Korean version of the wok—a soup kettle, rice tub, and a handful of cleavers. The heart and soul of Korean food is *kim chee* which is served as a side dish with every meal and usually made with salted, fermented cabbage that is highly spiced with chili peppers, garlic, scallions, and ginger. Variations are made with *daikon* (a kind of radish found in Japan and Korea) or just about any other kind of vegetable.

Traditionally the biggest meal of the day is breakfast, consisting of soup (some of which can be fiery hot), rice, fish or beef, and at least five side dishes with different vegetable and

Korean Rice Tea

Koreans love short-grain sticky rice, and inevitably a layer sticks to the cooking pot. When dinner is served, just enough water is poured back into the pot to cover the rice sticking to the bottom. This is allowed to simmer throughout dinner. After dinner, the rice-water tea takes the place of our after-dinner coffee.

tofu combinations as
kim chee.
Unlike both Japan
preferred by Koreans
stickier glutinous rice,
supposed to remain on
the Korean meal is
both millet (the only
and wheat in the form
make appearances.
Recently the
been exposed to the
Korea through their
specialties such as
want to truly savor the
a Korean restaurant
brunch on the
an amazing variety
prepared for *hot* food!

well as the ubiquitous

and China, the rice
is a sweeter and
and the rice bowl is
the table. While
centered around rice,
grain native to Korea)
of noodles also

Western world has
spicy flavors of
marinated barbecue
bulgogi but if you
cuisine of Korea, find
that serves a buffet
weekend, and sample
of tasty treats. Be

Excuse Me

In China, Japan,
and Korea, belching
discreetly after a meal
is considered a
compliment.

Hand to Mouth

*T*he Vietnamese underwent nearly a thousand years of Chinese rule—plenty of time to impose Chinese manners. But, to the amazement of most historians, the Vietnamese took what they found beneficial (including chopsticks), rejected the rest, and managed to maintain their own proud and distinct culture. (Some historians suggest that the tendency of Chinese emperors to post their most ineffectual relative to the faraway province of Vietnam may have had much to do with this phenomenon.)

That opportunistic characteristic is aptly reflected in the eating style of Vietnamese today. Before the arrival of the Chinese in 111 B.C., the Vietnamese ate with their hands. In fact, in many of the high mountain villages of Vietnam that the conquering Chinese ignored, people still eat exclusively with

The Soul of Vietnam

One explanation for the impressive resistance of the Vietnamese to being absorbed into China was the extraordinary adaptability and power of village customs. They would borrow from the Chinese at will—readily accepting chopsticks and improved agricultural methods but never forgetting that the soul of the people resided in the ancestral village. That character is encompassed in the ancient Vietnamese saying, "the king's laws bow before village customs."

their hands today.

For most of the country, how ever, chopsticks, along with the Chinese spoon and the tradition of eating out of the central pot, were a welcome but not exclusive addition. Vietnam is the only chopstick- wielding country that regularly and comfortably integrates the chopstick style with eating by hand.

In Vietnam, many of the most prized dishes (such as *cha gio*) involve plucking cooked ingredients out of a central pot with chop- sticks, placing them onto a rice-paper pancake or a vegetable leaf, followed by hand-rolling, dipping, and eating. The Vietnamese also have a broad selection of *dim sum*-like concoction, (such as *Banh Cuon*) that are simply dipped by hand into sauce and eaten.

Chopsticks in the Kitchen

In China, stir-frying is usually an energetic affair accomplished with a ladle. The Vietnamese concluded that a pair of cooking chopsticks—heavier and longer than those used to eat with—was more suited to their version of stir-fry. One reason might be that the relatively small amount of oil used by the Vietnamese requires a less dramatic utensil to do the job.

Delicate Cuisine

At first glance a plate of Vietnamese food might look a lot like Chinese food, but that impression will disappear after the first taste. In fact, the essence of Vietnamese cuisine may be best understood in contrast to Chinese food. Politically Vietnam spent centuries resisting the dominance of Chinese culture, and that resistance finds full expression in Vietnamese food.

Where the Chinese love to use generous portions of peanut and sesame oil, the Vietnamese go to incredible lengths to avoid using any oil whatsoever. Where the Chinese love to stir-fry and deep-fry, the Vietnamese prefer to simmer, steam, or eat food raw.

Virtually everything about Vietnamese food is light and delicate, with lemongrass, shallots, scallions, mint, coriander, and the subtle *nuoc mam* sauce taking the place of Chinese bean pastes, ginger, sugar, vinegar, cornstarch, and soy sauce.

While rarely appearing at a Chinese table, fresh, uncooked vegetables and salads are an integral part of most Vietnamese meals. Even the Vietnamese pancakes, used to roll up spiced meats, shredded vegetables, and fruits for dipping, are different. They are made of rice flour and pounded so thinly you can read the newspaper through them.

As the French, who took a brief turn learning about the indomitable Vietnamese spirit, say, Vietnamese cooking is the nouvelle cuisine of Asia.

The flavor of Vietnam

What soy sauce is to China, *nuoc mam* is to Vietnam—the essential flavor that underlies the cuisine. *Nuoc mam* is made by piling layer after layer of salted anchovies and other small fish into a wooden container and letting this mixture ferment in a cool, dark corner. The light, brown liquid that runs off is *nuoc mam*. Properly made it has an exquisite and delicate flavor, and is used in almost every dish imaginable, as well as being set on the dining table in a role similar to table salt in the West.

The second most-used sauce in Vietnam—usually for dipping food—is *nuoc cham,* which is just *nuoc mam* with ground chili, garlic, vinegar, sugar, and lemon or lime juice added.

Chopstick Diplomacy

While the adoption of chopsticks forced the Japanese, like the Chinese, to focus more time in preparing food so that it could be eaten in bite-sized pieces, the Japanese imposed their own traditional sensibility on the process. And the results on cooking and eating are distinctly Japanese.

From the start, the Japanese rejected two Chinese fundamentals—the spoon and the common pot. Soup remains a vital feature, but it is served in a lacquered bowl and lifted to the mouth. The central pot still exists but is reserved for special dishes such as *Sukiyaki* and *Nabemono*. For the most part, Japanese food is heavily compartmentalized, with each person receiving a separate dish for each component of a meal.

Emily Post-San

Here's the official etiquette for beginning a Japanese meal, as proscribed by the Ogasawara method. You first remove the lid of the rice bowl with your right hand, place it in your left hand and then set it down on the left side of your tray. Then follow the same procedure to remove the lid of your soup bowl. Then, lift your chopsticks horizontally from the tray with your right hand, transfer them to your left hand and then back again to your right hand. Then pick up your rice bowl, transfer it to your left hand and (finally) eat two mouthfuls of rice.

This procedure continues throughout the meal, never eating or drinking from any particular dish more than twice without a chopstick full of rice in between. In this manner, each bite taken will be fully appreciated.

In Japan, chopsticks are the only utensils allowed at the table, and preparation thus became even more crucial than in China. The Japanese met this challenge by raising food preparation and table manners to an art form. Indeed, when the first cookbook was written in the sixteenth-century, it flatly proclaimed that all cooking and eating begins and ends with chopsticks!

While this might have been somewhat of an overstatement—*Sushi*, for example, is meant to be eaten by hand—it was not much of one. At around the same time as the first cookbook, the Ogasawara system of manners was developed; it started with clear instructions on the proper way to begin each meal with the ritual picking up of the chopsticks.

Ladling Soup with Chopsticks

The Japanese have an expression for trying to understand an idea that is either hopelessly confusing or complicated: "understanding what you are saying is like ladling soup with a chopstick."

Samurai Cooking

The Japanese reaction to chopsticks was to focus attention on the individual pair of chopsticks when they are full of food. Not only is the flavor important, but also the appearance. In order to assure that each dish is not only perfectly cooked and flavored but also pleasing to the eye, the Japanese kitchen relies upon a much broader array of equipment.

Replacing the multipurpose Chinese cleaver is an assortment of specialized knives, ranging from a kitchen carver and a tofu slicer to an almost endless variety of fish and garnish knives. Pots and pans range from rice tubs (special deep pots for boiling rice), steamers, casseroles, cast-iron pots, and skillets to more specialized tempura pots and omelet pans.

Historically, the basic ingredients of Japanese cooking were dictated by what was available on the islands. Rice, fish, assorted soybean products, and seasonal local vegetables made

Zen Meets Cooking

Zen Buddhism has had a profound effect on all aspects of Japanese culture including cooking, yet while the cuisine of Japan is simple and elegant, it doesn't totally adhere to the ideas of Zen cooking. According to *The Essence of Zen Cooking,* the good Zen cook must be one with mushrooms when he meets with mushrooms, one with turnips when he meets with turnips, and so on. And the three "don'ts" of Zen cooking are: don't spend money when cooking, don't be luxurious, don't buy anything. Tough advice for a Western chef.

up the bulk of most meals. The flavoring of dishes is simple, relying primarily on soy sauce, fish stock, and sake, with sesame seed, shiitake mushrooms, assorted seaweed, vinegar, and horseradish used for variety.

Unlike most other cuisines of the world, there is a tendency in Japan to prepare and serve each ingredient separately, thereby accentuating the unique look, flavor, and texture of each part of the meal. A typical meal will consist of a bowl of *miso* soup garnished with a few small cubes of tofu and a sprinkling of sliced scallions, an individual bowl of rice, a dish of pickled vegetables, grilled or steamed fish, and anywhere from two to five dishes of assorted vegetables or slightly marinated salads. Every item will be beautifully arranged in a separate dish with an *eye* to the look as well as the taste.

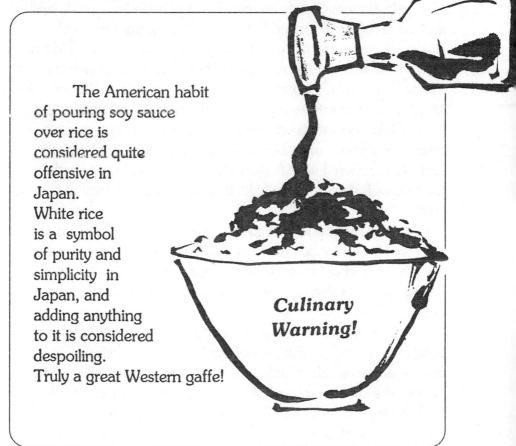

The American habit of pouring soy sauce over rice is considered quite offensive in Japan. White rice is a symbol of purity and simplicity in Japan, and adding anything to it is considered despoiling. Truly a great Western gaffe!

Culinary Warning!

The Stuff of Sticks

Bamboo is the reigning king of chopsticks. Cheap, plentiful, easy to splice, resistant to heat, impervious to boiling oil, and without any perceptible taste or odor of their own, bamboo chopsticks have dominated the world of Asian cooking for centuries. But while most Asian kitchens still rely on bamboo to do the yeoman's labor, the chopsticks that make it to the table have been fashioned out of virtually every kind of material conceivable.

In ancient China, chopsticks of ivory, silver, gold, jade, and coral regularly graced the tables of emperors and rich landlords. Jade and ivory chopsticks were highly regarded not only for their beauty, but because their polished surface helped to cool hot foods. However, they were particularly slippery, and users risked the embarrassment of dropping food all over the table. Gold chopsticks were symbols of wealth, but as symbols often are accompanied by burdens, in this case the preening rich often suffered sore fingers after struggling to manipulate the unusually heavy chopsticks through an entire formal banquet.

The Japanese, true to their centuries-long fascination with wood, fashioned chopsticks out of virtually every kind of tree they could get their hands on, including cedar, cypress, willow, pine, mulberry, ironwood, sandalwood, ebony, and birch.

The Japanese are also responsible for the object of so much frustration on the part of novice Western chopstick users—lacquered chopsticks. First developed during the early part of the seventeenth century, these chopsticks are made by pouring layer after layer of lacquer onto a prepared wood or bamboo chopstick and then polishing to a smooth and slippery surface. The lacquered chopsticks of today's Japan, complete with intricate inlays and colorful designs, are beautiful to look at but leave many first-timers struggling mightily to get a single grain of rice into their mouths. The elegance and durability of lacquered chopsticks, however, make them a favorite for special gifts, and for personal chopsticks designed to last a lifetime. They range in price from approximately $3 a pair for the decent mass-produced type to as much as $100 for a handmade custom pair.

The Wajima Nuri area of Japan is famous for making chopsticks with between 75 and 120 separate layers of lacquer; each layer is then hand-polished to a fine finish. When completed these chopsticks are said to be harder than metal and can be passed down through a number of generations.

Choose Your Weapon

With a design as basic and simple as chopsticks, it is hard to imagine too many variations. But with three millennia to think about it and four different cultures applying themselves to the task, the result is a dazzling array of chopsticks.

The basic types divide easily among the four centers of chopstick use:

In China, the people's chopstick is approximately nine inches long, round or square at the top end, and round and thick at the eating end—solid, heavy-duty tools.

The Vietnamese use unmodified, Chinese-style chopsticks. While they accepted chopsticks as a part of the thousand -year Chinese occupation, they refused to expend any energy contemplating improvements.

At first, the Koreans simply took the Chinese version and thinned it down a little, but once they had mastered the art of metal work, things changed quickly. Today Korea is the only country in the world that routinely uses metal chopsticks.

I'll Have a Pair in Eight-and-a-Half

The Japanese have determined that the proper length of a custom pair of chopsticks is exactly 1.2 times the distance from the tip of your middle finger to the base of your palm. Hopefully for your sake that is nine or ten inches since those are the standard sizes manufactured today.

Haiku Miso

Once you become skilled at the use of chopsticks, you will earn the right to complain about the most difficult food to eat with chopsticks. For some it is rice, for others the slippery noodle, but the ultimate test is if you can pick a tiny square of tofu out of a bowl of *miso* soup—not enough pressure and it drops back in, too much pressure and the tofu crumbles to pieces.

The Japanese started out with bamboo chopsticks that looked like tweezers and were connected at the top. That concept fell out of favor quickly and the Japanese finally settled on an elegant design—shorter than the Chinese chopstick by an inch or so, thinner all around and tapered to a point at the eating end.

Each country has also developed its own specialized variations within the general style. There are slightly longer chopsticks designed for serving; even longer and more sturdy cousins for the heavy-duty work in the kitchen such as stirring, flipping, and dipping into hot oil; special two-foot-long monsters for deep-fat frying; and even long metal or metal-tipped chopsticks for rearranging burning charcoal or wood.

For the hungry consumer, perhaps the best of the bunch is the difficult-to-find but well-appreciated Japanese noodle chopstick. Shaped like the standard Japanese chopstick but with a series of ridges carved into the eating tip, these chopsticks makes eating noodles the purely joyous occasion it should be—the ridges grab hold of the slippery noodles before they can slither off your chopstick and back into the bowl.

A Mountain of Chopsticks

The disposable chopstick was born in 1878 when a Japanese schoolteacher named Tadao Shimamoto found that while he had carefully packed a delicious lunch and brought it to school with him, he had completely neglected to include a pair of chopsticks.

Fortunately for Shimamoto the school was located in Yoshino County, which was famous throughout Japan for the production of high-quality cedar barrels. After explaining his predicament to one of the local coopers, Tadao Shimamoto was given a cedar sliver to carve into chopsticks.

History does not record exactly why he chose the method he did, but he carved the two chopsticks together attached by a small wooden bridge. The design is no doubt familiar to anyone who has eaten in a Japanese or Chinese restaurant, for Tadao's hunger-driven carving created a sensa-

Be a Culinary Environmentalist

The bamboo pair of chopsticks that came with this book can last you through many years of good eating and can be your regular companion whenever you dine at a restaurant that might try to force a pair of disposable chopsticks on you.

Make yourself a small holder (or if you are lazy use a clean child's sock) so after use you can stuff them back into your pocket and wash them at home. Bamboo will withstand dishwashers and just about anything else, but the best way to clean them is with a gentle rinse of soapy water.

Samurai Foxes

If you were to go on a picnic in Japan today and use disposable chopsticks, it is likely that after lunch your hosts would carefully break the chopsticks in half before throwing them away. This custom stems from a belief arising in the thirteenth century among early Samurai warriors that if the then-plentiful Japanese foxes were to gather up one thousand intact pairs of discarded chopsticks, a thousand foxes would be changed into human beings and a thousand Samurai warriors would be transformed into foxes. By breaking chopsticks used outdoors, the warriors continue to be protected to this day.

tion of commercial activity in the local area which began turning out disposable chopsticks—called *wari-bashi*—in large numbers.

It is unclear whether or not Tadao Shimamoto shared in the profits that rolled in from the rapid spread of disposable chopsticks, but he certainly receives his share of appreciation. Each year representatives from the disposable-chopstick manufacturers and marketers of Japan gather at a shrine in Shimamoto's hometown to perform a disposable-chopstick ceremony in honor of the father of the *wari-bashi*.

Down With Disposables

*J*apan was the source of the disposable chopstick, and it is fitting that Japan now leads the world in environmental resistance to them. In fact, the first active resistance to throw-away chopsticks arose in Japan in the late 1930s. With the onset of World War II other issues took over center stage, but the anti-disposable sentiment broke out again in 1972 as a spontaneous campaign of housewives in Sapporo.

More recently, environmental groups such as the Japan Tropical Forest Action Network have led the struggle to

return to a reliance on reusable chopsticks. About half of the disposable chopsticks are produced in Japan, and the remaining half are imported from China, Indonesia, Korea, and the Philippines. Estimates vary greatly, but Japan alone uses somewhere between 13 and 25 billion pairs of disposable chopsticks each year—which represents somewhere between 120 and 200 million cubic meters of lumber a year, enough to build over ten thousand homes. Lately, disposable chopsticks have become a symbol of disdain for the environment in Japan, and increasing numbers of Japanese have taken to carrying their own personal chopsticks to restaurants in order to avoid using the ever-present disposable variety.

Bugs in the System?

On the day after Christmas in 1984, while Europeans and their New World descendants were polishing their silver forks, knives, and spoons after the big Christmas meal, the general secretary of the Chinese Communist party was exhorting the six hundred million citizens of China to toss away their chopsticks and buy themselves a nice set of silverware.

While it sounds today like a truly harebrained idea—trying to throw three thousand years of distinguished chopstick history out the window—in fact Hu Yao Bang had his reasons and they weren't all bad. For decades China had suffered recurring outbursts of deadly infectious disease, particularly hepatitis, and much of the rapid spread of the disease had been

Imperial Manners

During the Ch'ien Sung dynasty of fifth-century China, a custom arose dictating that the emperor eat with two spoons and two sets of chopsticks. In that manner, he could serve himself with one set and eat with the other. Since there was always too much food served for the emperor to eat, the remains, kept clean by the serving chopsticks, could be eaten by the servants. This was said to be the precursor of serving utensils.

traced to the combined effect of the traditionally shared pot of food with the use of chopsticks, both as a way to get food from the pot and also as the means to deliver it to the mouth.

The result was that anyone at the table infected with any contagious disease quickly passed it to everyone else. Hu Yao Bang—the first Chinese Communist party leader to discard the Mao tunic in favor of the Western suit—concluded that abandoning chopsticks and promoting individual servings would go a long way toward wiping out infectious diseases.

This idea didn't go over very well with the Chinese people. Hu Yao wasn't just suggesting a change of table manners, he was attacking the

very core of the
Chinese family. During
the day the family might be scattered,
working hard at their daily chores, but at
dinner the family gathered around the table with
chopsticks flashing and conversation at a high pitch.
Not even the Chinese Communist party could stand up to the
power of chopsticks.

The Rise and Fall of Japan?

According to the *New York Times,* Japanese social scientists have theorized that the "economic miracle" of the Japanese economy can be directly attributed to chopsticks. According to this theory, the pivotal factor is the extraordinary dexterity Japanese toddlers are required to master in order to eat. Years later when those children become factory workers, that manual skill translates into the edge of quality that has helped Japanese products rise from the days when "made in Japan" meant cheap to a hallmark of excellence.

If there is any merit at all to the theory, the Japanese are now in serious trouble. In the early 1980s the Japanese Ministry of Education did an exhaustive survey and discovered that over 40 percent of elementary school children failed at basic chopsticks technique. Even more alarming was a later study that claimed that nearly one-third of folks over thirty, while managing to get food from the table to their mouths, were routinely butchering the classic style of chopstick usage.

Things got so bad in Tokyo that the police department started having training sessions on chopstick use for new recruits—only they first had to convince them that the real reason

The Ubiquitous Burger

While social critics and educators worry about whether or not the traditional Japanese love affair with chopsticks is in danger, the Tokyo location of McDonald's continues to sell more hamburgers each year than any other single outlet in the world—and no, you don't get chopsticks with your Chicken McNuggets.

was to elevate their level of manual dexterity so they would be better police officers!

When the Ministry of Education's report hit the news, it caused a minor whirlwind, with commentators, politicians, and self-appointed cultural purist all apportioning out blame for the sad state of chopstick-ability. First in line for abuse were the new generation of Japanese parents. Critics pointed to the appalling explosion in sales of the ugly but utilitarian two-headed utensil (fork on one end, spoon on the other) as the symbol of lazy parents unwilling to force their precious children through the ritual torture of chopstick training.

It is true that chopstick use is on the decline. The most probable reason is the internationalization of the Japanese family and restaurant cooking. With almost half the food now consumed in Japan tracing its roots to some other country (including multiple millions of McDonald's hamburgers), chopsticks are not so necessary. A counterattack on this trend is now being mounted by the Japanese school system which has incorporated chopstick usage into the curriculum, and it is unlikely that chopsticks will ever lose their central place at the Japanese table. But it is also probable that as Japan expands out into the international community, chopsticks will never again reach the level of importance they once had.

The Imperial Connection

So completely did chopsticks work their way into the hearts of the Japanese that they appear in a place of honor in many of Japan's religious ceremonies, including the single most important ceremony—the coronation of a new emperor. The ceremony, know as *Daijo Sai,* began over 1300 years ago in the year 673, shortly after chopsticks appeared in Japan. The first emperor to perform the ceremony was Temmu, an important figure in the early attempts to centralize the government of Japan. The ceremony has continued to this day without interruption whenever a new emperor is crowned, most recently on the occasion of the new emperor Akihito in 1989.

The *Daijo Sai* ceremony begins at midnight on the night before the coronation. As a part of the ritual, the emperor-to-be makes an offering to the gods—with an unadorned pair of pure willow chopsticks—of a portion of the new rice of the year and sits down twice during the night and eats with the gods.

The ceremony ties together the favor of the gods, the welfare of the emperor, and the hopes of the people for prosperous years to come. After the coronation, the emperor annually repeats the ritual with the year's new rice crop, expressing thanks for the bountiful harvest and requesting favorable treatment in the year ahead.

At the same time the emperor performs this ritual to ensure a prosperous year for the country, there is a public gathering at the Kasuga Shrine in Nara to pray for the happiness of the emperor and his family. At the ceremony four very large pairs of chopsticks are presented to the gods to eat with, and two human-sized pairs are used by representatives from the emperor and the people.

Perhaps the high point of the year is August 4, Chopsticks Day. At a large shrine in Tokyo, the priests who tend the shrine bring out two ritual pairs of nearly four-foot-long chopsticks, and people from all over come bearing used pairs of chopsticks. After considerable music and dancing, the old chopsticks—as many as 20,000 pairs at once—are burned while the people express their thanks and appreciation for all the chopsticks used in the past year.

Shinto: A Religion of Awe

Shinto, the native religion of Japan, is unlike most other religions in that it has no real gods and does not preach a particular set of moral values. It is instead based on an appreciation for the mysteries and wonder of nature. An extraordinary mountain peak, a twisted tree, oddly shaped rocks, or just about anything created by nature that evokes a sense of awe is honored, frequently with a shrine. At the heart of Shinto is a sense of communion with and reverence for nature that echoes throughout Japan's art, architecture, cuisine, and even the extraordinary beauty and variety of wooden chopticks.

Baby Magic

Perhaps because they come in pairs and are crucial to a central social function in Chinese society—eating—chopsticks have come to play an important role in the Chinese wedding.

Traditionally chopsticks were an obligatory gift—usually from the husband's parents—and were given to ensure that the couple stayed together happily and produced many children. Sometimes to assure a particularly close marriage, the wedding chopsticks would be carved with a picture that began on one chopstick and concluded on the other. These chopsticks were usually wrapped closely together with a bright red ribbon (for good luck) and accompanied by two rice bowls.

If by chance the wedding chopsticks failed to produce the expected offspring, there was an alternate method. Each year on the 15th day of the first lunar month, a childless couple could sneak into the home of a prosperous neighbor with many children, and steal a pair of chopsticks. The newly acquired chopsticks, having already proven their ability to bring forth both children and wealth, would no doubt result in a steady stream of babies.

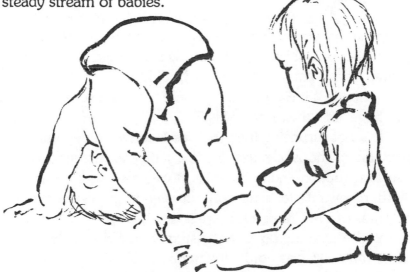

Wedding Warning!

Chopsticks are traditional gifts at both Japanese and Chinese weddings, symbolizing togetherness, the hope of a lasting cooperative marriage, and of course the anticipation of many a fine meal to be shared. But with the invention of disposable chopsticks a new taboo was born—don't give disposable chopsticks as a wedding gift! Since they are meant to be split apart and thrown away after being used once, they can only bring a quick demise to a newlywed couple.

Morality Sticks

*F*or the Chinese, after centuries of struggling with food shortages, everything associated with a meal takes on broad symbolic significance. The phrase *chun gao bing,* loosely translated "Have you eaten?" is the traditional manner of greeting friends. Similarly, when people lose their jobs, they are said to have "lost their rice bowls."

It is not surprising then that, as a common denominator at every table, chopsticks became the symbolic yardstick to measure corruption and decadence. It was okay to be a rich landlord, magistrate, or emperor, but even in the very undemocratic times of the Chinese Empire it was always wise to remember who paid the taxes, and using chopsticks made of precious materials was borderline behavior at best.

One of the earliest recorded laments at the failure of certain leaders to understand this basic principle came from one of history's great chopstick standard bearers, Chi-tzu, uncle to the last emperor of the Shang dynasty, and later, under the name of Ki-ja, the probable founder of chopstick culture in Korea.

Chi-tzu saw the emperor's use of ivory chopsticks as a sign of incredible decadence and was recorded in the ancient Shih-chi records as having complained to his emperor-nephew, "Now you are using ivory chopsticks, next you will want to drink from a jade cup, then you will want to own rare animals from distant countries; it's a slippery slope towards luxury and extravagance."

Chopsticks as a measure of moral purity surfaced again in the ancient Chinese novel *The Scholars.* The hero, Fan

Chin, a dedicated local boy who successfully completed the arduous training to become a Mandarin administrator, returned to his home village and had a banquet thrown for him by the county magistrate. Finding a pair of silver inlaid chopsticks at his place of honor, Fan Chin refused to sit down. The magistrate quickly replaced

them with an ivory pair but Fan Chin would not budge. It was not until a simple bamboo pair of chopsticks were placed before him that he agreed to sit at the table.

Steadfast in his youthful incorruptibility, only the simple bamboo chopsticks of the people could satisfy Fan Chin that he at least would not be corrupted by the silver and ivory symbols of wealth.

Chopsticks Save an Empire

Perhaps the most fondly remembered emperor of China was the founder of the Han dynasty, Kao-tsu. Born a commoner named Liu Pang, he participated in the rebellion in 206 B.C. against the crumbling and corrupt Ch'in empire and convinced the remnants of the Ch'in hierarchy to surrender the capital without a fight.

Originally just one of many leaders of the rebellion under the overall direction of Hsiang Yu, Liu Pang increased in popularity through his policy of sharing credit with his military leaders and treating both the common people and his enemies fairly and with compassion. At the same time, Hsiang Yu lost all support through his own cruel arrogance and eventually committed suicide in total isolation.

One of Kao-tsu's first acts as emperor was to drastically reduce taxes—always a popular move—but the delicate calculations of how much tax the government actually needed to maintain a strong defense and social stability were somewhat of

Chopsticks as Counters

The story of Emperor Kao-tsu and his chopsticks led to a saying that is still common in China today—"using chopsticks as counters." However, its meaning has changed slightly. Whereas at Kao-tsu's table the chopsticks represented taxes to be collected, today the expression refers to the practice of having someone stand in for someone else.

a problem.

During an evening meal, his chief minister, Li Shih-ch'i, was suggesting a tax plan when they were joined by a friend named Chang Liang. Chang saw that Li's scheme was doomed to fail and borrowed a handful of chopsticks to lay out on the table as counters to graphically demonstrate the error of the idea.

After gazing at the chopsticks a moment, Kao-tsu spit out his food and scolded his minister, saying, "You worthless bookworm, you came within a chopstick of losing me my empire!"

Chopsticks of War

The Empress Jingu Kogo is a legendary figure in Japanese history. According to the lyrical accounts of her accomplishments, chopsticks played an important role in her life. Known as the Woman Warrior of early Japan, she is said to have prepared for her fleet's successful invasion of Korea by spreading chopsticks over the ocean as an offering to the sea gods to ensure a safe and successful passage across the hundred mile straits to the shores of Korea. Because of her feats, the empress is revered even today by the Japanese navy as their patron saint.

Historians have a slightly different version of events. The Japanese interest in Korea stemmed from Korea's strategic position between Japan and China. The Japanese were hungry for a continued flow of the wonders—like chopsticks—that filtered down through Korea from China. However, the fiercely independent Koreans weren't about to be conquered—at least not for any lengthy period of time—by anyone.

Fortunately for the Japanese, the Koreans spent a considerable span of their early history fighting among themselves. At the time, there were three competing kingdoms, and the Japanese were able to gain and maintain a foothold on the Korean peninsula through a creative alliance with the southern kingdom of Paekche. It is likely that Jingu Kogo's fleet was welcomed to Korea as an ally of the people of Paekche, and that the Japanese participated as brothers-in-arms for at least one of the many battles between Paekche and the kingdoms of Koguryo and Silla to the north.

Woman's Country

The earliest known Chinese references to Japan referred to it as "Queen's Country." Indeed, many if not most of the legendary leaders of Japan prior to the arrival of the Chinese were women. Many historians claim that in its earliest history, Japan was a society dominated by women. By the seventh century, however, even though the last of the woman empresses was still on the throne, they had become mere figureheads. The influence of the male-dominated Chinese culture won out, and women were relegated to their current position of near-total subservience.

The Sacred Willow

In Japan, most of the ceremonies require the use of chopsticks made from the willow tree. This is because the willow tree is the first tree in spring to bud, and because its pure white wood complements the traditional Shinto desire for ritual purity.

A Bridge to Buddha

One of the most interesting and important religious figures in Japanese history was a Buddhist monk named Kukai. Kukai had sailed in 804 to China as a part of the recurring cultural
excursions, and returned, after spending many years in China, with a missionary zeal.

Kukai is largely credited with transforming Buddhism in Japan from its then-lofty but limited role as a philosophy of the aristocrats to a widespread religion of the people. He accomplished that deed by integrating all the local Shinto gods and ceremonies into his version of Buddhism; and in fact the history of Buddhism and Shintoism became so interwoven in Japan that it was soon impossible to tell where one ended and the other took up. While Kukai was out campaigning for Buddhism, he was just as actively promoting the use of chopsticks. In an effort to get the common people to use chopsticks, Kukai not only travelled like the Johnny Appleseed of chopsticks, handing them out to anyone and everyone but he also told people that if they used chopsticks, Buddha would help relieve the stress and suffering of their lives.

His methods were unorthodox but effective. Kukai is celebrated today as one of the first truly populist figures in Japanese history—concerned with equality and the fate of the common person. Kukai's methods have been carried on by faithful disciples ever since, and every October fifteenth, the Chopsticks Temple at Tokushima Shikoku founded by Kukai hands out chopsticks to all comers as a bridge to Buddha.

A Chinese Lottery

After the final crumbling of the three-centuries-long T'ang dynasty in the year 905, China was thrown into a period of confusion. The south broke up into warlord states, known as the ten kingdoms, while the north, the traditional center of dynastic power, stumbled through a number of short-lived dynasties, none lasting more than twelve years. Called the Five Dynasties period, it was one of the low watermarks of Chinese history.

None of the emperors had the power or the will to bring the southern warlords under control, the traditional harassment from nomads of the north was escalating into a threat to overwhelm all of China, and the nominal rulers of China seemed content to live in luxury and squeeze out what taxes they could from the people.

Busy Busy Chopsticks

Some historians speculate that this poem by a famous Ming poet was a social commentary on the plight of the servant class in China:

Busy, busy bamboo chopsticks
First to taste sweet or bitter
It is others who savor the food
And you who wing back and forth in vain

Ch'eng Liang-huei
Ming dyansty

Most of the emperors thrown into and then out of power came from the remnants of old imperial families and were ill-prepared to lead an already splintered nation. One particular emperor, named Yin Ti, could not even figure out how to select the best ministers for his government, so he placed the names of all the eligible scholars in a vase and pulled them out at random, position by position, with a pair of chopsticks.

Unfortunately the chopsticks proved less adept at selecting ministers of state than at selecting delicious morsels from the banquet table, and Yin Ti's rule lasted less than three years.

The Secret Life of Chopsticks

Throughout history, the rise and fall of dynasties in China followed a cyclical pattern. A strong ruler would emerge, overthrow the rotten shell of the last dynasty, and rule with an eye toward improving both the stability of the land and the life of the people. Gradually, as successive emperors lived in the rarified atmosphere of the palace, they lost touch with the concerns of the population and grew soft and decadent, ultimately to be overthrown by the next strong ruler.

It was in the later years of the social deterioration during the eighteenth- and early ninteenth-century reign of the Ch'ing dynasty (also known as the Manchu) that the secret societies, known in the West as "triads," began to grow in strength. While their political philosophy was blurry at best, their opposition to the decadent Manchu rule and their harkening back to the populist days of the early Ming dynasty garnered them wide popular support.

Organized more on the model of the Mafia than a political party, the triads mixed a peculiar blend of extortion, protection rackets, and popular political activism. They possessed an almost paranoid obsession with secrecy—secret membership, secret passwords, secret languages, and, of course, secret codes.

The simplest and most commonly used code was the chopstick code. In every village or neighborhood, a designated messenger—usually a shopkeeper easily visible to all passersby—would signal triad members by the simple placement of his chopsticks on his bowl or tray at the end of the meal. The signal would mean: tonight we are meeting at our regularly designated time and place.

Undoubtedly chopsticks played an important role in
mobilizing the triads for the massive Taiping Rebellion in 1850
that disrupted all of northern China
for a period of fifteen years and
is generally acknowledged
as marking the emergence
of China into the
modern era.

Golden Chopsticks

Chopsticks of metal—even precious metals like gold and silver—are rare in Chinese history. There are differing theories as to why this is so. Many people believe it stems from the long-held tradition, developed from centuries of political intrigue and competing warlords, of never placing knives on the table. While metal chopsticks are not exactly knives, they could conceivably accomplish the same task. Others simply point out that metal is not nearly as pleasing to the mouth as bamboo or ivory.

Whatever the reason, around the year 730, Sung Ching, chief minister to the great T'ang emperor, Hsuan Tsung, found himself less than thrilled when the emperor presented

Eatable Gold

Tofu originated in China over 2,800 years ago in the middle of the Chou dynasty, but didn't make its way to Japan until sometime in the 12th century. It is so packed with protein that it is often called the meat of the Orient. Tofu is made by soaking soybeans, then reducing them to a mash and boiling them in water. Vegetable oil and lime juice added, and the paste is stirred until it starts to foam. It is then placed in a press and all the liquid is squeezed out. When it cools and solidifies, the liquid becomes tofu. The remains of the soybean mash can be eaten, but by then it has been stripped of all its nutritional value. In Japan, at least, it more often ends up as floor polish.

Little Devils

Golden chopsticks may have gotten all the attention from the wealthy, but the common people had their own precious chopsticks. Historically the Japanese believed that chopsticks made out of mulberry, camellia, or willow were charmed, and if used by children would rid them of their devilish behavior.

him with a pair of golden chopsticks at a specially-called spring wine feast. Sung Ching, known throughout the land for his attempts to rid the palace of intriguing parasites, his steadfast opposition to capital punishment, and his interest in the well-being of the common man, was unsure how to interpret the peculiar gift. But upon being reassured by the emperor that the gift signified that Sung Ching was as straight, upright, and precious as the golden chopsticks, he gladly accepted.

Golden chopsticks also made an appearance in the early Chinese novel, *The Dream of the Red Chamber*. A peasant girl, invited to dine at a feast of a local wealthy magistrate, is given golden chopsticks to eat with in a act of pretension. Not used to the extraordinary weight, she has difficulty manipulating the heavy chopsticks and drops a pigeon egg onto the floor, thereby disgracing herself and providing the novelist with a measure of tragedy.

Additionally, golden chopsticks have been discovered in Korean sites dating from the Han dynasty (around 2,000 years ago) and were recorded as in existence in 15th century Japan when the Shogun Yoshimasa—a figurehead who ruled in place of the emperor—thanked his closest advisors with a gift of golden chopsticks.

Safe with Silver

From very early in Chinese history, silver chopsticks were used, sometimes as everyday eating chopsticks but more often as testing and serving chopsticks. They were reputed to offer protection against one of an emperor's worst fears—assassination by poison.

Very little could disturb an emperor more than the thought that, after rising to a position where the culinary delicacies of the world were his to be enjoyed, he could easily be done in by a small dose of lethal poison. Silver chopsticks were widely believed to turn black at the touch of any poison, thereby saving the life of the emperor and dissuading potential assassins from attempting to spoil a good meal. So servants of the emperor would test each of his dishes with silver chopsticks before he ate, thus ensuring his continued life. The emperor

Protection Only Goes So Far

Yang Kuei-fei, the grandest femme fatale of Chinese history, always used a pair of chopsticks made from the rare horn of the rhino. They were supposed to protect her from her many enemies. This concubine spent a good number of years as the power behind the aging Emperor Hsuan Tsung's throne and is generally credited—undoubtedly more than she deserves—with initiating the decline of the T'ang dynasty in the late eighth century. Unfortunately for Yang Kuei-fei, her rhino chopsticks did not protect her from being strangled and tossed in a ditch by angry supporters of the emperor who blamed her for all his troubles.

A Well-Omened Touch

Ancient Chinese folklore claims that people who use three fingers to manipulate their chopsticks are easygoing by nature, while those who use four fingers are well omened. And those who manage to fit all five fingers onto the chopsticks and still keep them under control are destined for greatness.

himself would not use silver chopsticks to eat; the feel of metal in his mouth was considered distasteful. A little after-the-fact scientific checking has demonstrated that silver will indeed turn black after contact with hydrogen sulfide—released by rotten eggs, onions, or garlic—but isn't phased by the more garden variety assassin tools such as cyanide and arsenic. All in all, it is likely that many more chefs suffered the emperor's wrath than would-be food assassins.

Even in the later Ch'ing dynasty in the eighteenth century, when the imperial household shifted from silver chopsticks to ivory, they ordered silver markers to be inserted into each dish—better safe than sorry.

Bribing the Gods

*E*verywhere in the world farmers are renown for their willingness to try anything to improve their harvests. The farmers of Japan are no exception, and chopsticks play a major role in their efforts.

In many areas of Japan farmers annually carve a pair of chopsticks out of chestnut (reputed to have a calming effect on whoever uses it) for the local gods responsible for rice production and invite these gods into their homes to eat with these chopsticks during the fallow months of winter. Not wanting to offend the gods in any way, the chopsticks offered are usually inordinately large. Come early spring the gods are sent back into the fields, hopefully mindful of the honor paid them.

Traditionally, not all farming areas, however, were willing to trust the annual crops to such an unorganized feast. In the area of Niigata, for example, farmers have an annual cere-

Scare Tactics

Not willing to trust their fate entirely to the gods, inhabitants of the Nagano farming area of Japan hold a special ceremony every October 10th to pray for an abundant rice crop and include in the ceremony the scarecrow that guards over the all-important family garden. As part of the ritual, the scarecrow is given a pair of long chopsticks carved out of the white radish called *daikon*.

mony to which the gods are invited. There 280 pairs—perhaps representing the length of the growing season—of god-sized chopsticks (nearly two feet long) are presented. In prudent farming fashion, however, all 280 pairs are not made each year. Instead the old chopsticks are shaved down to make then appear fresh until there is not enough wood left. Only then are new pairs made.

The Problem of the Long Reach

Chopsticks have proven themselves to be a remarkably versatile tool for the table, but not without sticky problems to overcome. Perhaps the most troublesome problem over their long history has been the user's urge to reach for food in the serving dish after the chopsticks have just been used, thereby facilitating the spread of disease.

The Koreans have two straightforward solutions—they customarily either serve everyone individually or use a serving spoon. The Japanese tend to serve everyone individually also, but they still do have meals served in common dishes. And for the Chinese and Vietnamese who don't use serving spoons and generally prefer eating together at large tables, the problem had to be addressed in other ways.

In the early 1980s the Chinese Communist party made a brief and comical attempt to get citizens to abandon chopsticks in favor of knives, forks, and spoons (see page 50). A more simple solution that has frequently been promoted and infrequently used is to supply an extra set of serving chopsticks either for each person or for each plate or bowl of food.

The government of Taiwan, demonstrating that the Communists have no monopoly on failed chopstick reforms, recently launched The Plum Flower Campaign, so named because it was supposed to convince the people to set their table in the shape of the plum flower—with an extra serving pair of chopsticks at each place. So far, the campaign has failed.

Unfortunately, the germ theory has only been around for a fraction of chopsticks' illustrious history, and ancient habits die hard. One Chinese explanation

for why Chinese chopsticks are longer than Japanese chopsticks proudly exclaims that it allows you to reach farther across the table to get to a morsel of food.

Until custom catches up with science, one approach that is catching on with a matter of politeness, in use particularly in Japan, is to use the reverse ends of your chopsticks when selecting food from the common pot.

Tea Master

The Japanese tea ceremony is known all over the world and is often seen as a reflection of traditional Japanese cultural values—elegant, ritualistic, and simple yet perfect as to form. Ironically the tea ceremony, as created by the venerable tea master Sen No Rikyu, began not as a formal ritual, but as a celebration of the pleasure of sharing with friends a simple meal of seasonal vegetables topped off with a good cup of tea.

What is not commonly known outside of Japan, is that Sen No Rikyu's tea ceremony began with hand-carved chopsticks for each of the participants. On the morning of the ceremony, Sen No Rikyu would carve a pair of chopsticks from Japanese cedar for each of his guests, knowing that they would all appreciate the fresh smell and delicate touch of the newly shaved cedar and would take delight in the beautiful red grain of the chopsticks.

Today few people take the time to carve chopsticks, but before a tea ceremony cedar chopsticks are soaked in ice water

From the Tiny Acorn . . .

Throughout Japan there are many trees that are said to have grown from chopsticks. According to the legends, when great men stick their chopsticks into the ground, a sacred tree that embodies the spirit of the man will grow from the used chopsticks. The missionary monk Kukai is credited with numerous trees. Undoubtedly any tree grown from the chopsticks of Sen No Rikyu would be a particularly elegant cedar.

to approximate the
color and texture
of freshly
carved cedar.
The chopsticks
used for the tea
ceremony are tapered
on both ends, just as
Sen No Rikyu first
carved them, and are
appropriately called
Rikyu bashi, or
Rikyu's chopsticks.

Hanging by a Thread

*I*n the earliest days of international commerce, of all the spectacular wonders coming out of China one of the most impressive was the light and luxurious bolts of silk. Few people outside the silkworm-growing villages ever knew that the unassuming chopsticks played a key role in the early development of the silk industry.

The early production of silk from the "little darlings," as the silkworms were called, began in spring. The excitement level of the small silk-producing villages raised perceptively with the first buds of the all-important mulberry trees. The tiny black silkworm eggs were then spread out on strips of cotton and watched carefully until their color, in tune with budding leaves of the mulberry trees, began to change to shiny green. At this point the women of the village would wrap the cloth across their bellies and retire to their sleeping mats to carefully await the incubation of the little darlings.

Once hatched, the worms were placed on trays in a warm shed and feed a constant diet of mulberry leaves. As the worms grew bigger and bigger their appetites increased until the activity of the village consisted entirely of stripping trees of their leaves and pouring them onto the silkworm trays. You

Girlish Giggles

The Japanese expression for girls at that "certain age": She's at the age where she giggles at the drop of a chopstick.

80

could barely hold a conversation within hearing range of the silkworm shed for the noise of worms eating.

If the village was lucky the worms would begin to weave their cocoons before the mulberry leaves gave out, and finally, in a good season, the shed would be covered in bright, silky white cocoons. Then the hard work of harvest would begin, and it was here that chopsticks played their crucial role. The women of the village would split open the silkworm cocoons and carefully reach in with a finely tapered pair of chopsticks to pull out the silk filaments. Using just the right pressure so as not to break the delicate strands, they would use the chopstick to draw out the silk by twirling the chopstick around like a small reel. From there the silk would be woven into cloth.

Unfortunately for our hero, the Chinese soon invented a more specialized silkworm reel and chopsticks were sent back into the dining room.

Mastering Chopsticks
The Foolproof Method:

*L*earning how to use chopsticks with grace and ease is not—despite all indications to the contrary—a difficult task. For those of you who have tried to decipher the miniature instructions with the funny illustration of a scrunched-up hand that come printed on some disposable-chopsticks wrappers, fear not—the secret of chopstick ability will now be revealed.

There are many different ways to hold chopsticks, but by far the easiest is the classical method described below and recommended in numerous Chinese and Japanese etiquette books down through the ages. These instructions are written for right handers; if you are left handed, you'll need to make the translation.

One caution before you begin—some people learn by reading and looking

at diagrams, some by listening and others by doing. So if after you have read through the following surefire directions, studied the illustrations, and tried to do it, you are still having

#1

difficulty, have a friend read the instructions to you one at a time while you apply your fingers to the task.

1. Hold your right hand up straight in front of you with the palm facing sideways, to your left. Place one chopstick in the crook of your thumb and forefinger about an inch down from the top of the chopstick. Make sure it is tucked all the way down in the crotch of your thumb and held firmly by pressure from your thumb. (See illustration 1.)

2. Place your ring finger against the chopstick and exert just enough pressure to hold the chopstick steady. (See illustration 2.) If you wiggle your hand around you will see that because of the pressure of your thumb and ring finger, the chopstick will move only in conjunction with your hand.

#2

3. Move your hand back up straight, with the chopstick still firmly held by the base of your thumb and ring finger, and bend the top half of your forefinger and middle finger back toward you. (See illustration 2.) You are now ready for chopstick number two.

4. Rest the second chopstick on the pad of your thumb (not the very top, but not too far down, either) and bend your forefinger and middle finger down to rest on the chopstick. Make sure your forefinger is on top of the chopstick running

along its length, with your middle finger playing a supporting role along the backside of the chopstick in the same way you would hold a pencil. (See illustration 3.)

5. The secret to using chopsticks is that the bottom stick remains fixed and unmoving at all times. You need to use only very slight pressure from your forefinger and middle finger to open and close the tips of your chopsticks, by bringing the top one down or up and around whatever delicious morsel you have selected.

6. If this is your first time, you will probably find that the tip of one of your chopsticks is extending out farther than the other. The simplest way to rectify this *without* having to start all over again, is to hold the tips down on your plate or table-top, and loosen your pressure on the chopsticks just enough to let the short one slide down to the plate. Then reassert the pressure and start eating.

Classic Error #1:
Wandering Middle Finger

A common error in execution is the migrating middle finger. You get all set up, with the bottom chopstick firmly held and your fingers properly set up on the top chopstick and then as soon as you turn your head, your middle finger slips from the backside of the chopstick to the bottom. The next thing you know, you can't get the tips back together because your middle finger is blocking the way.

Some people find that trying to put all the pieces to-gether feels very much like trying to rub your stomach and pat your

#3

head at
the same time,
and they experience difficulty
shifting attention back and forth—
concentrate on one finger and another
finger slips off.

The system described above should solve these problems if you make sure you get the bottom chopstick set first. Once you've got your thumb and ring finger holding it in place, all you have to remember is to not let up the prressure while you focus on the more tricky top chopstick.

Classic Error #2:
Chopsticks Death Grip

Many novices try *so hard* that they end up causing more and more tension in their hand. The result is cramped fingers and a general inability to open and close the chopsticks. Try to remember that chopsticks are just little sticks and—as long as you are not trying to use pure gold chopsticks—are very light. They can and should be manipulated with only slight pressure.

Chopsticks for Cheaters
(or Small Children)

This is *not* a substitute for learning how to use chopsticks, and cannot really be used as training chopsticks since it does not operate in the same way. This method can, however, help make small children not yet ready to master the real item feel more included. Besides, it's a neat trick to impress your friends.

Find a piece of paper and fold it down into a small wad about half an inch thick. Place the paper between the chopsticks about one inch from the top. Dig out the rubber band that you have been carrying just for this, and wrap it around the chopsticks on both sides of the paper, but particularly tight at the end.

If you did this right, you should

Classic Error #3:
Five-Fingered Finesse

It is possible to hold and manipulate chopsticks using all five fingers, but you had better be really good and have very small hands. The sad truth is that for most people, there is simply no place in the chopstick grip for your little finger, and if it insists on joining in it will end up bunching up your hand in a way that makes it impossible to get the tips of the chopsticks together.

Classic Error #4:
Choke Hold

For some reason many chopstick virgins intuitively believe that the farther down the chopsticks you hold the easier it will be. Actually the opposite is true. The farther your hands move toward the tips, the less leverage you have and therefore the harder you have to work. Move up toward the top and you'll find easy going.

end up with chopsticks that look like the illustration here. Then all you have to do is push down to close and let up to open. If these chopsticks are for you instead of your child, just remember that the Japanese used

tweezer-like chopsticks for a couple hundred years before abandoning them, so don't feel too bad.

Chopstick Taboos

All four of the chopstick-wielding countries have rules of chopstick etiquette. For the most part they are similar, but the Japanese have the most elaborate set of "do's" and "don'ts." This list is culled—without embellishment—from the traditional etiquette tomes of Japan:

Do not eat with a broken or mismatched pair of chopsticks.

Do not begin eating without greeting others at the table (except in Korea where there is usually no one else at the table and you are supposed to be quiet).

Do not eat twice in a row from the same dish (except your rice bowl, which doesn't count).

Do not hover over dishes trying to decide what to take.

Do not dig under food with your chopsticks to get the best pieces. (A Chinese addition would be, do not eat food directly from the central pot—transfer it to your plate first).

Do not lick your chopsticks.

Do not eat with your face bent over the plate like a dog.

Do not push food directly into your mouth from the bowl. (In Korea, do not even lift your rice bowl off the table.)

Do not search for food in your soup.

Do not stab your food with a chopstick.

Do not touch food with your chopsticks without eating it.

Do not use chopsticks as toothpicks.

Do not hold chopsticks in your mouth while using your hands.

Do not scratch your head with chopsticks.

Do not stick chopsticks in your rice.

Do not set chopsticks on you bowl of dishes (chopsticks should be placed on the table, chopstick holder or tray—in Korea you can, however, put your used spoon in your soup bowl).

Do not make noise with your chopsticks.

Do not put chopsticks up your nostrils.

Do not point chopsticks like a knife.

Do not reach across another person with your chopsticks.

Do not finish your meal before anyone else.

Bottoms Up!

Throughout the Far East, it is considered impolite to refill your own glass—particularly if you are drinking alcohol. Your task and that of your drinking partners is to constantly be aware of the other person's glass and be ready to refill it. If you don't want any more, leave a glass partly full and be prepared to fend off at least two tries to refill it.

Big-Time Taboos

Some taboos are worse than others. By far the worst are those commonly associated with religious ceremonies and funerals. Sticking chopsticks down into a bowl of rice (as colorfully illustrated on the cover of this book) is commonly done at funerals, as an offering to Buddha, or as an offering at an ancestral shrine. It also reminds the Chinese of incense sticks used at funerals. Therefore it is not supposed to be done at other times. Another serious faux pas in Japan is to pass food from chopsticks to chopsticks. Not only is it unsanitary, but it reminds the Japanese of the funeral ritual of passing amongst the family the bones of a cremated relative.